"Roger is a compassionate, ca
wants to use him. His book ﹍﹍ ﹍﹍
reminder that hearing and obeying God would produce God's fruit. Not only is his story a blessing to those who have received financial help, but also to anyone who wants to honor God with their finances. When I was starting a new NGO, Nehemiah Global Initiative, for North Korean refugee work, we were in financial need for the start-up cost, we prayed and asked God to provide and shared with a few people about our needs for the new initiative. When Roger heard our ministry's need, he also heard the voice of God telling him to give, and he simply obeyed even though it was a number outside his comfort zone. It turned out to be the exact number that we have been praying for at that time. Through his obedience, we were able to start the NGO, and many lives are being saved, restored and cared for. His book clearly demonstrates that obedience requires faith, and faith in action would produce God's results. I highly recommend this book for anyone who wants to obey God's will, and for God's will to be done through his or her life."

— KENNETH BAE, FOUNDER AND PRESIDENT,

NEHEMIAH GLOBAL INITIATIVE

"Roger Lam is honest and transparent in sharing his financial journey that led him to understand the difference between money and riches.
Read the book and make this life-changing discovery for yourself."

— CHUCK BENTLEY, CEO, CROWN FINANCIAL MINISTRIES

AND AUTHOR OF *MONEY PROBLEMS, MARRIAGE SOLUTIONS*

"Roger's personal journey that he shares with such vulnerability is an anointed piece of work. His honesty, humility and grace is evident in every page as he aligns himself to the character of Christ – namely His humility, His unselfishness and His faithfulness. I found Roger and Sylvia's story gently speaking into my heart, teaching me through real life experience and scripture that our Father God is indeed the owner of everything!"

— CRAIG DEALL, CEO, FOUNDATIONS FOR FARMING, ZIMBABWE

"Roger Lam finds joy in giving. Now he's giving to you. In *Lost and Found: Money vs. Riches*, Roger shares his story and his soul. His transparency will make you uncomfortable... and then comforted. You will love Roger's heart and—more importantly—love the Father's heart as He leads Roger on a journey to freedom and joy. Roger has taken the lessons it took a lifetime to learn and distilled them into a quick, gripping page-turner. Every giver should sit down for an hour with Roger, and stand up refreshed, renewed, and ready to walk in deeper faith."

— CAMERON DOOLITTLE, SENIOR DIRECTOR, GENEROSITY PATH

"I was honoured to meet Roger and his wonderful wife Sylvia at the Christian Economic Forum in Singapore. I was struck by the genuine Christlike love that they exuded. I could see they were not playing at being Christians. These were real Christians with big hearts. Roger's book about his stewardship journey reflects the Christlike big heart that God transplanted within him. True personal testimony always speaks louder than anything else because it's real and true and honest and from the heart. Testimony from the heart speaks to other hearts. Roger's testimony spoke to mine."

— BEN FREETH MBE, ZIMBABWE

"*Lost and Found: Money vs. Riches* is a gripping read. I opened the book thinking I would start with a couple of chapters, and didn't put it down until I had finished it. This is not a conceptual book on 'how to handle money', but one that takes us on a real-life journey of learning to trust God with our finances in our day to day. Roger's vulnerability in sharing the details of his own struggles draws us in, and the end result is both refreshing and inspiring. Over the years, Roger has passionately shared many of these stories in our church, and I've witnessed not only his growth, but a growth in our members as a result of his faithful sharing. This book is for all of us who want to honor God with our money. I recommend you read it, share it and then share your own journey so that together we can grow in glorifying God with the handling of our money. Thank you Roger for leading the way!"

— STEVE GAULTNEY, SENIOR PASTOR, COMMUNITY CHURCH HONG KONG

"I'm grateful to Roger for sharing his story with us and know that it will be both a blessing and challenge for anyone who picks it up. He writes, "Psychologists say that everyone has a love language; mine was money." Later on he writes, "I led a life that was driven by fear and anger, and I suffered." He is transparent, gritty, humble and candid regarding his relationship with money and, by God's grace, the ensuing redemption and transformation in his life. You won't want to put it down and I believe you'll find it to be a very worthwhile investment of time."

— DARYL HEALD, FOUNDER, GENEROSITY PATH

"Pick it up! It's a page-turner! With a unique blend of humor and humility, Lam reveals that money had wormed its way into the corners of his life leaving him stuck. Only when he followed the teachings of Jesus on the handling of finances, did he find himself on a pathway to freedom. In plain terms, Lam helps us see that we don't figure out what Jesus is trying to teach us until we live it out. He wants us take hold of life! It's a modern-day Pilgrim's Progress for anyone in business, financial services or whom God has entrusted any measure of money. You won't put it down."

— GARY HOAG, PH.D., GENEROSITY MONK /
ECFA INTERNATIONAL LIAISON

"As Rogers' cousin, I have been a passive bystander to Roger's life, witnessing subtle changes in his character through sporadic family dinners over the years. This book has provided much insight into how these seemingly gradual positive changes required so much faith, effort, pain and had such an inspiring back story.

I believe most of us deep in our hearts believe basic theories such as "giving to others makes one happy" or "being rich does not equate to being successful". However using our own lives and own money to test these theories requires a whole new level of bravery and faith. Yet Roger has done just that. This book is almost a personal case study to 'prove' the above true and hence has set a blue print for young aspirers of 'success' such as myself. Whether a believer of Christianity or not, this book is a great source of wisdom and a great read for anyone seeking the 'truth'."

— AARIF LEE 李治廷, ACTOR / SINGER

"Growing up with Roger, we used to refer much to the film series Star Wars, mostly by association with the 'dark side'...

How warming and honoured it is to have witnessed the turn of a man, newly born, cleansed by God's grace and the blood of Jesus Christ.

Roger's simple and authentic sharing empowers those who are bound by fear and anger to break through the shackles that hold us back from receiving the fullness of God's love for us.

Lost and Found: Money vs. Riches starts with the lens of money, but it is so much more on how God touches Roger's heart, and hopefully as we read it, all of us too."

— David Liao, CEO, HSBC China

"Captivating is the way I would describe this book. From the opening page to the last paragraph, I was riveted by the honesty and transparency of the author. As you journey with the author through this story, you will be encouraged, inspired and convicted. Encouraged to know, God does delight in the cheerful giver. Inspired to be more generous. And, God will likely use this book to convict you because you will be reminded that Jesus says more about how we view and handle money than about any other topic—including both Heaven and Hell and prayer and faith. If you apply the principles found in this book, your heart will be aligned with heaven's priorities... 'for where your treasure is, there will your heart be also'!"

— Tom G. Mangham, Sr. Vice President,
Organizational Development,
Evangelism Explosion International

"In this personal and poignant narrative, Roger Lam unfolds with deep honesty the challenges facing his life and the impact of God in leading him to the limitless, generosity of His Kingdom. This is a brave book for a financier to write at all but especially to a world where greed goes unchecked.

It is a story of liberation, a liberation that we need: to be free of the controlling influence of money and materialism.

Jesus was utterly clear, we cannot serve God AND 'mammon' - an apt word for modern financial acquistion!

In each intimate chapter, Roger reveals the tough and loving journey that God has been and still is taking him on, in order to liberate him from the life of performance and acquisition that had trapped him at every point. I recommend this book to be read carefully and meditatively.... The message is deeper than the words."

— MARTIN RADFORD, CEO, INNER CITY MINISTRIES, HONG KONG

"Blessed is the man who believes, trusts in and relies on the Lord And whose hope and confident expectation is the Lord.

For he will be nourished like a tree planted by the waters, That spreads out its roots by the river; And will not fear the heat when it comes; But its leaves will be green. And it will not be anxious in a year of drought Nor stop bearing fruit."

JEREMIAH 17:8-9

"Thank you, Roger, for the courage to be honest and vulnerable before both God and men. Your moving testimony helps us confront the deception of our hearts, and spurs us to choose faith over sight, generosity over bondage, heavenly over earthly treasures, and divine wisdom over human intelligence. There is no greater encouragement than a man who has chosen to trust and plant himself in God and His word of truth come rain or shine, through the harvest and the drought. We cannot wait to read your exciting next book as God continues to unfold His incredible plans for you and your precious family."

— JOYCE AND HENRI SAMOUTOU, FOUNDERS, NEW SIGHT CONGO

"My friend Roger Lam has written a fine book on an important subject. Most of us struggle with money: will we master it or will it master us? Roger shows us, from his own life experience, how to make money our servant in Christ. You are going to enjoy this book."

— THE HONORABLE GREGORY W SLAYTON, CHAIRMAN, FELLOWSHIP OF FATHERS FOUNDATION AND FAMILY FIRST GLOBAL

"*Lost and Found: Money vs. Riches* by Roger Lam is a book that just had to be written. I for one am grateful that God used what most of us would regard as painful circumstances, the loss of a job, to make the time available for Roger to put his thoughts down on paper - or should I say a laptop. Ironically, for me, it is this change in personal circumstances that gives this book extra credibility. As Roger says, it is easy to write 'when the sun is shining down on me, and the world's all that it should be'. But to say (or sing) Blessed Be Your Name, we also need to experience 'pain in the offering'.

This book makes it very clear that generosity has little to do with finance but everything to do with attitude. God is extraordinarily, extravagantly generous. James 1:5 SAYS He 'gives generously to all'. If God is so generous to us, we also should 'always be generous'. In John 3:16, at the heart of the gospel, God GAVE. Christ's life and teachings reflect this, as Roger so clearly shows us in this book, Jesus had a lot to say and demonstrate about generosity and clearly expects His followers to do the same.

I loved Roger's real-life stories which he has shared humbly and not in any way out of a sense of boasting. I praise God for the times He has filled Roger's heart with compassion (I really appreciate his honesty in the times he 'tried to make a deal with God' - the Kenneth Bae story was quite amusing!)

I remember reading that it is compassion which is the gateway to generosity. I am reminded of the compassion (literally from the gut!) exhibited by the Good Samaritan in the famous Bible story, I see it reflected page after page in this excellent little book. A word of caution, it would be dangerous for someone to read this book and decide to 'do' generosity. It is not a project, but a lifestyle. Roger has faithfully adopted this lifestyle, at the same time as being refreshingly honest that he, like all of us, is still on a journey, still learning - as we are inspired by the lifestyle of Jesus. But it is a journey that liberates us, fills us with joy, connects us with others and finds us making investments in the things that really matter.

In a society that so often sets itself up by encouraging us to 'get rich', I pray that you will read this book and that the Holy Spirit will lead you to discover, as Roger has, the Kingdom relationships and purposes that our generous and loving Father is leading you to share your resources with. After all, He is a 'Good Good Father', Jehovah Jireh who knows our needs before we even ask.

Bless you and your dear family, Roger. Well done good and faithful servant."

— JOHN SNELGROVE, FOUNDING SENIOR PASTOR,
THE VINE CHURCH, HONG KONG

"In I Timothy 6:10, "For the love of money is a root of all kinds of evil." In Ecclesiastes 10:19b " ....and money is the answer for everything." How should we, as Christ's believers, try to strike a balance between not being preoccupied by the desire of possessing this "root of all kinds of evil" but at the same time, be a good steward and use it for the glory of God? Roger, in his journey of faith with Christ, lived out what it means to be totally set free from the bondage of money. Through his deepest hurt, Roger allowed God to turn his slavery to money into triumphant victory in gaining mastery over it. Throughout this book, he cited many miracles of how God demonstrated His sovereignty over, not only his life, but also everything he owns. He has been totally set free from financial bondage and now lives a life full of excitement, without knowing what lies ahead, but keep trusting God every step of the way. This is a book for every person who wants to be a better steward in Christ financially and I highly recommend it!"

— DR. GEORGE SO, CEO,
FULL GOSPEL BUSINESS MEN'S INTERNATIONAL FELLOWSHIP (HONG KONG)

"Roger's testimony is engaging. It grips and compels us in our own journey - a journey out of slavery, bound in anger over our perceived earthly material inheritance, because of our "flawed revenue models"...towards freedom in Christ as we struggle to intentionally steward all that we have been blessed and entrusted with. As I read it, I've been compelled to reflect on the status of my own balance sheet of faith assets, stewardship liabilities and whether I've built sufficient equity toward honoring God in everything."

— COLLIN TAN, FINANCE CHAIRMAN,
METHODIST MISSION SOCIETY SINGAPORE

"Thank you for sharing the book, *Lost and Found: Money vs Riches*. What a wonderful job you have done in relaying your life story and tying in eternal truths from scripture. God has certainly touched you and honored your faithfulness to Him and I believe this book will be a great encouragement to many around the world as they experience the life-changing story of being freed from the bondage of money and in turn becoming rich toward God. I sense that God will you this book to change many lives and may you continue to be encouraged."

— WESLEY K. WILLMER, PH.D.,
STEWARDSHIP AUTHOR AND CONSULTANT

Lost and Found

Money vs. Riches

LOST AND FOUND

Money vs. Riches

"People are slaves to whatever has mastered them."

2 PETER 2:19

Roger Lam

ELM HILL

A Division of
HarperCollins Christian Publishing

www.elmhillbooks.com

Lost and Found
Money vs. Riches

Published in Nashville, Tennessee, by Elm Hill, an imprint of Thomas Nelson. Elm Hill and Thomas Nelson are registered trademarks of HarperCollins Christian Publishing, Inc.

Elm Hill titles may be purchased in bulk for educational, business, fund-raising, or sales promotional use. For information, please e-mail SpecialMarkets@ ThomasNelson.com.

Library of Congress Cataloging-in-Publication Data

Library of Congress Control Number: 2018936846

ISBN 978-1-595557476
ISBN 978-1-595557520 (eBook)

TABLE OF CONTENTS

An Invitation to Share a Journey from Slavery to Mastery

By Nury Vittachi

Money IS IMPORTANT. It talks. It burns a hole in our pockets. It parts itself easily from fools. It cannot buy me love. It excites us, draws us and enslaves us.

Yet there is a contradiction in our relationship with it. Studies repeatedly show that financial security is the single biggest worry that most of us have. Yet when we are asked to list the most important things in our lives, we don't even put money in the top ten.

Oddly, we worry about money way too much, and at the same time, we don't think about it nearly enough – not *deeply* enough. 'A wise person should have money in their head, but not in their heart,' said Jonathan Swift, the church minister who wrote Gulliver's Travels.

And that is where Roger Lam comes in. As a young person, money was an unhealthily big focus for him, as is probably true for many of us. Yet things changed for him in a marvelous way.

His journey transformed him and reading about it changes the reader, too. His story left me with the revelation that in a very real sense, every single one of us has exactly the same amount of money in our accounts. And that's not just a casual observation, but a life-changing discovery.

We also learn from him that it is really true that it is not getting money that makes you feel rich, but giving it away. Roger Lam's lessons on money can benefit everyone, but they are particularly valuable in Hong Kong, a financial city dominated by the movement of cash— and a place where people hate to talk honestly and openly about their personal financial challenges. By opening his diary, his heart and his pocketbook in front of us, Roger teaches us how to escape from being enslaved by the almighty dollar.

The truth is that money makes a terrible master, but a very good servant. Once you learn the practical truth of that, everything looks different.

Nury Vittachi
Hong Kong 2018

CHAPTER 1

HERO TO ZERO

CHANCES ARE YOU HAVE never heard of me. I am not famous, nor do I have a list of ultra-highflying achievements to show for my 24-year career in finance. My story may not resonate with you at all. I have no authority, and no qualifications whatsoever to write about the topic of biblical stewardship and generosity—apart from one thing: my personal story. My journey over the last 30 odd years was a struggle with money as the result of a childhood financial trauma which left me feeling poor, cheated, angry and exiled.

My name is Roger Lam, and I am a fourth-generation Christian. My grandfather was a co-founder of a church, and he also started a paint company, a well-known household brand in Hong Kong around the 1930s.

In some ways, we were an archetypal churchgoing family. As far back as I could remember, I had always gone to Sunday School with my parents, and I had always assumed that one day when I grew up I would take over the family business. We lived in a rented two-story house with a large garden in Kowloon Tong, a part of Hong Kong with tree-lined streets and relatively low-rise, stately housing: very different from the better-known parts of Hong Kong, with their crowded streets and neon lights. I had gone to the right kindergarten, the right elementary school and the right high school. I had a little talent in some areas, including oral English skills and tennis—and boy, did I know it. The kindest way to describe me at that time was arrogant.

My late paternal grandfather was possibly an overly generous man. Even though my dad was running the business, he was only given 10 per cent of the shares in the company, as the patriarch wished to spread his favors more widely. My granduncle and his sons collectively owned more shares in the company than my father did—which was where the roots of our troubles lay.

Our family nightmare began in 1985 when I was 13 years old. My granduncle and his sons brought in an outsider (a now deceased high-profile mainland Chinese businessman who had moved to Hong Kong) to do a hostile takeover of the family business that my father ran.

Even though I was very young at the time, I knew what was going on. My dad fought valiantly for more than a year, but he narrowly lost out to the other party.

He ended up having to tender his shares at a heavy discount. He had lost the company he had worked so hard to build up, and in his view, there was nothing left for him to do in Hong Kong. So, he decided to move our entire family to Vancouver in Canada.

At the age of 14, I was painfully aware, to the last penny, of how little money my dad had from the sale of shares, and from that point onwards I developed an insecurity about being provided for. I was an exile who felt that my birthright had been taken from me. I was angry.

CHAPTER 2

FEAR LEADS TO THE DARK SIDE

A WELL-MEANING family friend living in Vancouver suggested that my younger sister and I skip a grade because academic standards were perceived to be higher in Hong Kong than Canada. So even though the English language was not an issue for us, I ended up having one more issue to grapple with—I was a year younger than everyone else in my new environment.

It was difficult to focus. I wanted revenge so badly for what members of my own family had done to me. Success is the best revenge, right? Having no special athletic skills or other talents that would provide an easy alternative route to getting the big bucks, I thought the only way to go was to excel in academic results, and that meant going to a really good private school. However, at the back of my mind was a panicked feeling of worry about scarcity. My dad did not have any consistent income stream, and hence my sister and I ended up with no choice but to go to our local public school.

The first Christmas we spent in Vancouver was awful. I absolutely hated it. It was not so much Christmas that I hated *per se*, but my inability to take part in this festival of materialism in the way I would have liked. In particular, I hated Boxing Day sale in downtown Vancouver. Everything was on a big discount, and there was so much stuff that I had wanted, but the issue, of course, was MONEY! Some people had it. Though we had done all the right things, I was worried that our family did not have enough to keep up with the Joneses.

In my high school years, I ended up studying really hard to get good grades in order to make a name for myself and to break out from my money worries. I also did a lot of tutoring for my peers to earn extra pocket cash.

But teenagers are teenagers. At the time, I had a very challenging relationship with my mother, so I ended up going to a university as far away from Vancouver as possible. I moved to upstate New York, with the goal being to get as good a GPA in my studies as possible. My personality became very combative. In my view, you were either on my side, or you were The Enemy.

CHAPTER 3

THE LOST DECADE

G RADUATING FROM COLLEGE in 1993, I must have applied for something like 50 jobs, but I was rejected by 49 of them. Curt, unsympathetic people do not make good interviewees.

I think by the time I got to the final round interview in a couple of opportunities, the interviewers all seemed to have figured out that I had extremely low Emotional Quotient, and that I would not fit into their training programs. The only job offer I got was in Chicago, and at the time I had basically no idea what trading was about, and I certainly had no idea what a hedge fund was.

Yet once I got into place, things moved along smoothly enough. Looking back at those early years of work, I can see that the first 10 years of my career in trading, selling and structuring convertible bonds plus equity derivative products were relatively smooth sailing

in terms of getting paid and promoted—which was of utmost impor-
tance to me at the time. For example, thanks to a merger between a
Swiss bank which I had only recently joined and a UK merchant bank
in 1994, I was bumped up to Associate Director at the age of 22.

Two years later, when I was lured by a pay package of double what
I was earning together with the prospect of learning different aspects
of the equity derivatives business, I moved to another Swiss bank, and
within a year I was promoted to Director by the age of 25.

As a result of my childhood financial trauma, I took pay and
promotion very seriously. Psychologists say that everyone has a love
language; mine was money. In 2000, I started expressing my love for
my parents by taking care of their mortgage repayments for them.

Up to that point in my life, the Christian faith meant very little to
me—it was pure head knowledge. Since moving back to Hong Kong
in 1994, I started going to the 6 pm Sunday evening service at Union
Church because no matter how late I partied on Saturday, I figured
there was little chance I would still be sleeping on Sunday evening; I
was a sporadic churchgoer at best.

In early 2002, my parents recommended a new pastor at
Community Church Hong Kong, and I became a regular attendee
there instead. They had no evening service, so I had to get up on
Sunday mornings.

Back then, the church, known as CCHK, met at the glass-walled
75th floor apex of Central Plaza, a new skyscraper in Wanchai (it was

most likely one of the tallest churches in the world). Before the keyboardist would start playing the closing song, I would head out to press the elevator button, loathing to meet anyone at church, let alone staying behind after service to mingle and swapping small talk—I was scared that people might figure out what kind of person I really was.

A female member of the church was an ex-colleague from the mid-90s, and every time she saw me she would ask if I would go to her Life Group, one of a number of small cell groups where people from church gathered to study the Bible. I would smile at her politely and decline, but in the back of my head I would be thinking, "Lady, you have no idea what you're asking! There's no way I would go to your Life Group. If people even remotely had an idea what I was really like, I might even get kicked out of this church."

Despite being relatively successful at school and at work, I was unhappy. To quote the wise Jedi Master Yoda from the movie *Star Wars*: "Fear is the path to the dark side. Fear leads to anger. Anger leads to hate. Hate leads to suffering."

I led a life that was driven by fear and anger, and I suffered.

CHAPTER 4

WAKE-UP CALL

A PAIR OF life-changing events happened to me in 2003, more or less simultaneously. Had these two incidents not happened together, I would not be the person I am today.

I was working at yet another Swiss bank at the time in the area of corporate equity derivatives structuring, when I was bypassed for promotion to Managing Director. Disappointed, I ended up reporting to a peer based in Singapore.

Second, I was dating a girl very seriously, to the point that I had picked out a diamond engagement ring. Out of the blue, she decided to end our relationship.

If these two events had occurred separately, I may have had the strength to stomach it, but as a one-two punch it made me feel extremely low. That Sunday I went to church, and sure enough the same female ex-colleague from the mid-90s was there and asked me the exact same question: would you like to come to my Life Group? I was feeling miserable and desperate. I was already in the pits—what else did I have to lose? To her surprise, I asked for details of the meeting and promised that I would check it out. In hindsight, that was a gentle wake-up call that God used to get me back on track.

I was amazed to find that I soon felt I fit right in with that new cluster of friends. God blessed me with really wonderful Life Group members, hosts and leaders. They were not the judgmental people I had expected, and I started to look forward to attending Life Group to the point where I would adjust my work travel schedule to ensure I was back in town by early evening to attend the sessions.

The members in the Life Group became my extended family, and by getting to know the joys and trials in their lives, I started to realize that church is not a sanctuary of saints, but rather a hospital for sinners. I also learned what it means to "not think less of yourself, but to think of yourself less". There was a shift in my focus to start looking out for others' interests, as opposed to being purely self-serving. The Holy Spirit gradually softened and changed my heart to have God in the center.

So, the change started, bit by bit. I was helping with a Sunday service organized by our Life Group, visiting and handing out care bags to elderly discharged patients of a hospice, going to local hospitals to pray with members of the church suffering from serious illnesses, going to mainland China twice a year to visit orphanages in Beijing and Shijiazhuang, and so on.

Being a creature of comfort, it was very out of character for me to do all these things—my friends can testify to that! Subsequent attendance in programs like Alpha, Cleansing Stream and Walk to Emmaus helped immensely in reorienting my life towards serving God and becoming more like Jesus, serving in different ministries within the church.

CHAPTER 5

BABY STEPS

THE FIRST TIME I heard a full-length sermon on the topic of tithing was in 2005. I am a bit ashamed to admit that I was not deliberately following biblical teaching in any area at that point in my life. After hearing the sermon, I decided to start by being obedient in the area of money—which was odd, given my hold-on-tight attitude to cash. So why did it affect me? Possibly because (a) pay was relatively good at the time, (b) I was living with my parents, (c) I was still single, and (d) Malachi 3:10 was quoted during the sermon:

"Bring the whole tithe into the storehouse, that there may be food in my house. Test me in this," says the LORD Almighty, "and see if I will not throw open the floodgates of heaven and

pour out so much blessing that there will not be room enough to store it."

You take your 10% to God, and He returns so much blessing that you do not have room to store it. It sounded like a money-back guarantee. It was interesting that I did not recognize at the time that finance was actually my deepest psychological wound. Little did I know that this period would be the beginning of God's healing for me, turning my greatest weakness into my greatest strength.

I started to get serious about following God's teaching on stewardship, and naturally that started with the area of tithing. My pastor at the time suggested starting small, so I had no qualms following his instructions. And small it was: I started off with giving 1% of my base salary via autopay to church. This was back in the days when investment banking was still paying quite handsomely and, as mentioned, I was living with my parents, so I had no mortgage to pay. Handing over 1% was not exactly a challenge. The next month I tweaked the autopay instruction to 2%, and when that also did not move the needle, in the third month I bumped it up to 5%. As you can probably guess, by the fourth month I got to 10%, and I was feeling pretty smug with myself that I was now tithing according to God's instructions.

That year went by and then came bonus season. I thought to myself, "Am I supposed to tithe 10% of that? What about the unvested portion?" Long story short, after considerable thought I decided it just did not make any sense to play accounting games with God—you cannot hide from Him—I started to tithe on the upfront vested cash bonus for financial year 2005 and in the subsequent year the unvested stock awards as well. Truth be told, at the time there was a bit of muddled "prosperity gospel" thinking going on in my head. I was hoping God would bless me on the share price, since I had taken a leap of faith in offering Him my first fruits which had not even been delivered into my hands yet!

CHAPTER 6

BEYOND TITHING

IF I HAD previously been mistaken about having arrived, by 2007 I became even more convinced that there could be no mistake about that. I was serving on the church's council, co-heading the stewardship ministry at church, and fully tithing EVERYTHING!

I even figured out exactly where I ranked in the anonymous "league table" of church donations through some fancy analytics on the donation data. Just as I was gloating with spiritual pride, God gave me a wake-up call by telling me through different situations that there were some additional teachings of His pertaining to stewardship which I still needed to grasp.

My senior pastor at the time approached me after service one Sunday and mentioned there was a financial situation with a congregation member which he wanted to get my views on. A sibling in

Christ, whom I had always felt drawn towards but not known very well, had run into trouble with some loan sharks who had threatened this individual with bodily harm should the loan principal plus interest not be repaid in full within 72 hours (the sum amounted to 2.5 years' worth of this person's estimated wages).

At the time, I confess I did not know the Bible that well, but I vaguely remembered coming across concepts such as those in Galatians 6:2 and 6:10 to "carry each other's burdens" and "to do good to all people, especially to those who belong to the family of believers".

Looking straight in the eye of this helpless sibling in Christ invoked feelings of compassion, reminding me of the teaching in 1 John 3:16: "Jesus Christ laid down His life for us, and we ought to lay down our lives for our brothers and sisters." Having been blessed with a reasonably substantial amount of savings, I simply could not justify to myself how I could refuse to save this person from the risk of serious bodily harm—collectors of debts for loan sharks in Hong Kong can be frightening, violent people.

After asking a few due diligence questions to make sure that (a) this was the full amount required and (b) this debt was not a result of a gambling or drug habit, I cut this person a cheque on the condition that it was accepted as a zero-interest loan with monthly amortization, initially targeting a repayment period of 60 months. My sibling in Christ agreed to this as reasonable and doable. I did not know at the time that this was actually structured in accordance with Old Testament principles—Exodus 22:25 says: "If you lend money to one of my people among you who is needy, do not treat it like a business deal; charge no interest."

CHAPTER 7

HEART SURGERY

EVERYTHING WENT ACCORDING to plan in the first six
months. Repayments were on time, and this person got an additional part-time post which increased his earnings. Thereafter, the
repayments started to become a little bit more irregular. I deliberately tried to stop myself being vocal about the irregularity, thinking
that was not something Jesus would do. But in 2011, the repayments
stopped altogether.

There was much unintended food for thought out of this exercise
which had "seemed good to the Holy Spirit and to me" (referring to
Acts 15:28). It took some time before I mustered courage to gently
approach this sibling in Christ for help in understanding what was
going on. Was this individual making sufficient income to sustain
basic livelihood? We could lower the monthly repayment amount, and

thereby extend the amortization period to 10 years or more. Should I get angry with this person? Was I entitled to feel this way? Was I naively expecting repayment like clockwork? Was anything less than repayment in full deemed to be falling short of my expectations for doing a good deed?

The answers to these questions were found in the Parable of the Unmerciful Servant in Matthew 18:21-35. From an earthly standpoint, I had every right to be angry and disappointed, but from a kingdom perspective I plainly recognized that I was the servant who owed the king ten thousand bags of figurative gold, and I simply did not want to repeat the folly of choking my fellow servant who only owed me a hundred silver coins, especially after the mercy I had been shown by my Lord and Savior Jesus Christ.

There was no anger on my part, yet it was abundantly clear that the debtor was trying to avoid eye contact with me at church. Our relationship remained awkward and strained for some time, until I had an epiphany in 2014. It dawned on me that the loan was originally made in 2007—exactly seven years earlier—which meant that this was the Year of Debt Forgiveness for this particular non-performing, zero-interest, monthly amortizing debt! Deuteronomy 15:1-2 states: "At the end of every seven years you must cancel debts. This is how it is to be done: Every creditor shall cancel any loan they have made to a fellow Israelite. They shall not require payment from anyone among their own people, because the LORD'S time for canceling debts has been proclaimed."

My change of heart was only made possible through the power of the Holy Spirit, who enabled me to value relational reconciliation as a higher goal than reclaiming the money I had lent.

CHAPTER 8

NOT THERE YET

GOD HAS a great sense of humor. After every milestone, I would have a brief moment of thinking I had arrived, but without fail He would always show me the next leg of the journey shortly afterwards. If there is even the slightest hint that I am boasting about the progress I have made in my stewardship journey at all, I would like to make it unequivocally clear that all glory belongs to God the Father, the Son, and the Holy Spirit.

Shortly after the debt forgiveness episode, I became painfully aware that something was still not quite right in terms of my relationship with money: I found myself suffering from panic attacks during Christmas break in 2014, and the source of anxiety was money.

My income had been drastically reduced since it peaked in 2005-06 (to give you an idea, my total compensation was higher 20 years ago than it was last year), yet my giving in the form of parental support and so on had not proportionally decreased.

It was hard. My outgoings were bigger than my income every month. I was praying hard that my bonus would be sufficient to help me break even that year. Thanks be to God, the bonus that year exactly met that need.

It was evident to me that I had not arrived at a place of financial security and serenity yet. I was still pondering whether I was making and saving enough for my loved ones, even though this was long after I had built up a decent net worth, and having trained myself to stop seeking large price tag fixes of materialism (namely sports cars, mechanical watches and vintage wine). It actually brought me joy to skimp spending money on myself in order to be in a position to be generous to my family and to those in need. Praise be to God that this may be seen as a minor reflection of Christlike self-sacrifice beginning to be demonstrated in my life.

In parallel, our church wanted to strengthen stewardship teachings outside of the Sunday pulpit, hoping to avoid congregation members feeling that the sermon was a fundraising call. The Stewardship Committee decided to run the Crown Financial curriculum in late February 2015, and I volunteered to sit in the course so that I would be qualified to facilitate subsequent classes.

CHAPTER 9

FLAWED REVENUE SPLIT MODEL

THE PIN DROPPED after the introductory session. The very first verse that the guest lecturer quoted was Psalm 24:1: "The earth is the Lord's, and everything in it, the world, and all who live in it." I immediately figured out why I suffered from anxiety attack: I was on a revenue split model with God. The first 10% was His, and the other 90% was mine. How I saved it, spent it, invested it, and so on, was my business, thank you very much.

It was not that I had never heard what was said before, but it finally REALLY sank in that EVERYTHING I have belonged to God.

Naked I came from my mother's womb, and naked will I leave this world. I was reminded that I am merely God's fund manager.

What a relief that is! The 90% also belongs to God, and therefore every spending and saving decision is a spiritual one. God has promised to take care of all my needs (but not necessarily my wants), and let me tell you that is the most comforting thought in the world.

I had been so fearful of investing my hard-earned savings, with a chunk of it sitting in a US dollar cash account earning nothing over the last few years thanks to low interest rates. Through the Crown Financial Course, I was convicted that I had been the servant with one talent (please refer to the Parable of the Talents in Matthew 25:14-30) paralyzed with inaction due to fear of loss! There is much to repent from my financial history, but praise be to God I have now been set free by knowing the truth (John 8:31-32 says that "If you hold on to my teaching, you are really my disciples. Then you will know the truth, and the truth will set you free.").

From then on, I have had a progressive renewal in terms of my investment philosophy, increasingly seeing the need to generate greater returns, not so much for my own benefit but for the ability to give freely to situations which Jesus would move my heart to extend a helping hand. My fear of mark-to-market swings has also gradually reduced, knowing that at the end of the day it all belongs to God; and that He is Jehovah Jireh, the God who provides, recalling that He has never failed nor forsaken me all my life.

There is nothing more flawed than my view of work over the last 24 years that it is all about making money and getting recognition. I finally learned at the Crown class the proper perspective through which to see work: it is God's means of training our character, not a means of earning income. He takes care of our needs, not our earthly employer or our job *per se*. This refreshing perspective has enabled me to more fully view the workplace as a mission field instead of a battlefield, where God's principles matter infinitely more than Gordon Gekko's. In short, Matthew 7:24-25 says it best:

"Therefore everyone who hears these words of mine and puts them into practice is like a wise man who built his house on the rock. The rain came down, the streams rose, and the winds blew and beat against that house; yet it did not fall, because it has its foundation on the rock."

CHAPTER 10

DAUNTING INVITATION

I WAS INVITED to give my testimony at the CEO Forum in March 2015 (guess they ran out of people to invite given I was nowhere near being a CEO). What a day they chose. That morning there had been mass layoffs in my office, and it was a pretty emotional day. However, I realized that was not a good reason to put off an evening speaking engagement, and so I went. Little did I know, my dad was in the audience. He sat behind a pillar, so I did not even see him while I spoke. I told my story—the story you have read in the preceding pages.

I had never talked to him about this before. It was his moment to discover just how much his son had been impacted by having to grow up in the shadow of the lost family business. Guess I must have bottled it up inside pretty well all these years...

The very next morning, I received a very peculiar email. I

mentioned earlier that at church we brought in the Crown Financial course. I had had no prior contact with their organization, yet the email was from their CEO. It was an invitation to attend the 2015 Christian Economic Forum, to be hosted in Singapore at the end of August—just months away. He explained in the email that a few years back, he was curious how much God-content there was at the annual World Economic Forum held in Davos, and to his dismay after attending that conference, he discovered the answer was zero. It propelled him to start a parallel series with God in the center, and hence the name Christian Economic Forum, or CEF.

My first reaction was that this must have been a mistake or joke of some sort. I have done reasonably well in finance in my 20-plus years in the industry, but I was nowhere near qualified to go to Davos for the World Economic Forum, let alone its equivalent in Christendom. And so, I ignored the email for a while. During this time, it bothered me so much that I started speaking and praying about it with my wife and with my pastor, and in the end, I felt there must have been a reason for me to receive the invitation. Not knowing what lay ahead, I replied to accept the challenge.

I was a bit taken aback by how much it cost to attend this two-day conference in Singapore! Honestly, the thought of making up an excuse to decline did creep through my mind, but I thought to myself, "How lame would that be, Roger? Come on, you can afford it, just spend less on other things..." On top of that, I thought God must have had a purpose for me to attend this event. Participants were also given the option to bring their spouse along (at additional cost). In hindsight, deciding to bring my wife Sylvia along was one of the best decisions I had ever made (you will understand why shortly). So, I paid the conference fee to register the two of us.

Initially, I subconsciously overlooked a stated requirement. Each delegate had to produce a 1,500-word white paper on advancing God's economic principles in a few pre-selected areas (namely Economic Growth, Best Practices, Stewardship and Investing, Social Issues or Personal Growth). Writing a 1,500-word paper was something I had not done since college, but that was not the showstopper. What on earth is a *white paper*? I looked it up on Google, and to my horror this was the search result I got:

A white paper is an authoritative report or guide that informs readers concisely about a complex issue and presents the issuing body's philosophy on the matter.

It turned my stomach. I looked at the allowed topics, and there was absolutely nothing I had any authority to speak about. There was a May 15th deadline for the white paper. I could not understand why they set the deadline three and a half months ahead of the event.

I put the essay out of my mind. I had paid good money to go to this conference, so they could not possibly badger me to produce the goods, let alone in a timely manner.

The subsequent email correspondence with the organizing body shattered my naive assumption—they actually meant it. I asked for guidance on any acceptable sub-topics, samples of previous white papers, and so on, but it still did not help. I could not think of anything I could write about with the remotest sense of authority or credibility. Even though they extended the deadline to June 1st, that did not help either. I should have trusted my gut instinct that I did not belong, and I most certainly should not have paid the non-refundable registration fee.

Without even having chosen a topic by the extended deadline, I emailed the event coordinator with a lame excuse about having been really busy blah blah blah and asked for a further extension. I was given till June 15th to come up with something, with an implied caveat that they may ask for a rewrite if the draft was not up to standard.

Looking at the choice of topics again, I had the greatest affinity towards stewardship, I decided. However, everything that I had recently learned on the subject was from the Crown Financial Course (the organizer for this event). If I simply regurgitated the same teachings, that would not have only been lame, but that would have also made it clear to everyone that this fraudster just did not belong.

At the end of my ropes, I prayed to God asking for help, calling on Him to reveal to me what I was supposed to do. I heard this soft, distinctive voice telling me that I was indeed correct about my lack of authority to address any of the topics, but it said that I did have author-ity over my own stewardship journey. With that revelation, I cranked out the 1,500-word white paper in one sitting over a number of hours, which was essentially some of the earlier chapters of this book. That was all I had to offer, and I tried to put it down with unaccustomed openness and humility. The paper was submitted to the organizing body which accepted it with only minor edits. It was a huge relief, and I thought I could relax for the next two and a half months to quietly, uneventfully get this conference over and done with. Little did I know, this was the quiet before the storm.

CHAPTER 11

I'm Not Worthy

A FTER A QUIET period of about a month and a half, another email came, and this time it was even more daunting than the previous ones. What came through was 360 pages worth of all the white papers from each attendee, and the organizer wanted us to read them all before coming to the conference in order for us to discuss the ideas intelligently. Reading 360 pages in 20 days was not so much the issue (I divided the reading into 18 pages a day), but the daunting bit was finding out who was actually going to the conference.

The caliber of the attendees was exceptionally high, including some international guest speakers who had spoken at my church before. There were other participants from Hong Kong, and one name in particular stood out to me: this gentleman was so well-known in the Christian circles he even had a cable TV show on Christianity! Essentially, my gut instinct that I did not belong to this league was proven right, and after having diligently read through the 360 pages, my only wish was to have a quiet conference, get it over and done with, without being shown up to be the least qualified attendee.

Unfortunately, my nightmare just kept getting worse. Two weeks later came another email, and this one was more frightening than all the previous ones: I was asked to be a panelist to discuss stewardship. And guess who else was on the same panel? The cable TV show guy! I had never, ever typed an email reply so quickly in my life, trying to find out from the host what questions he was going to ask, and I promised that I would do a really good job to prepare for the answers (to save myself from embarrassment, which had been my biggest dread ever since I made the mistake of saying yes to this event). Sadly, the reply to my earnest plea took a few weeks, arriving just a few days before the conference. Instead of a list of questions on topics which I was desperately hoping to get a firm grasp of ahead of time, I was basically told that the participants will have read the white papers, and therefore the host did not want us to talk about our white papers on stage. Rather, he was looking for the panelists' rationale behind writing their papers.

Great, I thought. I had gone through all this trouble to pay a huge sum of money, sweat over coming up with this so-called white paper of mine, and then had to go up on stage and reveal to the global all-star team in Christendom that the reason for writing my paper was that I had nothing else to say. Lord, what had I done to deserve this, please?!

CHAPTER 12

MOCKTAIL CRISIS

WITH GREAT BUT rather anxious anticipation, Sylvia and I arrived at the conference site. In the evening before the conference began, there was a cocktail reception for all the delegates. We nervously walked into the beautifully decorated room located next to the garden in the back of the hotel for registration. The room was filled with spiritual giants from all over the world, and they all seemed to know one another—except Sylvia and myself, of course. I was desperately looking for a drink to calm my nerves, but to my dismay they only served juice, water and soft drinks!

Fifteen minutes into the extended small talk session, the host appeared and he mentioned that first thing the following morning when the program started, we were each going to introduce a preselected fellow delegate in the most honoring kind of way (in the spirit of Romans 12:10). Our task in the next hour was to find the person you were supposed to introduce, learn about his or her achievements, and to be interviewed by the person who would introduce you. I was determined not to fail at this seemingly easy first task at the conference. Driven by fear of embarrassment, I diligently went around the room to look for the person I was assigned to. After about 15 minutes, I started to panic. Having searched the whole room, I could not find that person. He was a local Singaporean delegate, and I figured that he must have decided to skip the pre-conference registration event. All I had prayed for was to not embarrass myself at this conference, which was clearly way above my league, and I was getting tripped up at this very first task! What was I going to do?

The search for this person continued after I alerted the organizers about the situation, and fortunately there was a brief biography in the stash of white papers for each delegate. When the mildly nerve-racking mocktail event was finally over, I went back to my hotel room and memorized this person's every achievement. In the morning, when it was my turn to present, I was able to deliver a masterful performance in pretending that I had spent the whole evening chatting with this individual and presented him in the most honorable way possible. He looked at me a bit funny while I did that (he was probably thinking I had never met this guy in my life), but never mind—I managed to avoid embarrassment at the very first hurdle.

CHAPTER 13

EPIPHANY

A FTER THE FIRST panel discussion in the morning, the host announced that he wanted everyone to bring out their smartphones to log on to a particular site. A bad feeling started to creep over me. "What now?" I thought. It turned out to be a voting app. To make things more competitive this year, the organizer decided to award the Best White Paper for each category based on popular vote.

Great, I thought, this is just what I needed. There was a gigantic screen behind the white lounge chairs on stage. I was imagining that votes would be tallied live shown on the screen, and next to my name a big fat zero. You can probably imagine how I was cringing at that point, lamenting my foolish decision in going through this ordeal.

At the end of that long and exhausting day, back in the hotel room Sylvia asked me what I was going to say at tomorrow's stewardship panel. I honestly had no idea. Once again, I found myself at the end of my ropes, and in my completely helpless state I went back to the ultimate source of wisdom through prayer. Recounting what I had learned on the first day at the conference, there was a panel discussion on Christian macroeconomics (do not ask me what that is about), so I thought it must be fair game to have Christian microeconomics, which is essentially what stewardship is about, deciding what to do with the money that is in your wallet based on biblical principles.

Suddenly, the answer to my prayer came through a question Sylvia asked me, "You've read all 360 pages of the white papers, was there any common theme or verse that jumped out at you?" Lo and behold, there was. Inexplicably, I immediately recalled seeing Micah 6:8 being referenced across a wide range of topics:

He has shown you, O mortal, what is good.
And what does the Lord require of you?
To act justly and to love mercy
*   and to walk humbly with your God.*

Then I started to think about the flow of my white paper, whether there was some way to tie it in with this verse. In the first part of my paper, I described my experience in learning to tithe during 2005-07. Spontaneously, Malachi 3:8 sprang to mind:

"Will a mere mortal rob God? Yet you rob me. "But you ask,
'How are we robbing you?'
 "In tithes and offerings."

Combining the two ideas, I rationalized that in money terms, to act justly is to not rob God in tithing. One down, two to go.

The second part of my paper was about the episode in granting the zero-interest loan to the sibling in Christ, then seven years later canceling the borrower's obligation to repay in the Year of Debt Forgiveness. I thought that could be a good enough proxy for showing mercy. Check. Two down, one to go.

In the last part of my paper, I talked about my mistake and repentance from the revenue split model with God. I did not think it would be too far-fetched to label that as walking humbly with God. Mission accomplished! Praise be to God! By His grace, I was comforted to have been blessed with something halfway intelligent to say at the panel discussion tomorrow, and with a big sigh of relief I went to sleep soundly.

CHAPTER 14

UNEXPECTED FINAL HURDLE

AFTER THE PANEL discussion host went up on stage for a solo presentation, all the panelists for the stewardship category were getting ready being miked up individually by the crew. Just as I was nervously waiting for my name to be called, I felt this terrible sensation in my stomach: I suffered from Irritable Bowel Syndrome, and nerves arising from the occasion triggered it off.

I was soon debating intensely with myself as to whether it would be wise to go to the bathroom at that moment, risk the mike being turned on and die of embarrassment even before getting on stage, or wait until later and risk having to dash off stage to relieve myself. "Lord, why?" I petitioned God. "All along I've only been trying to avoid embarrassment, and You have made me overcome all these hurdles, getting to this point with something remotely sensible to say on stage. PLEASE help calm down my bowels and save me from this disaster. After all, it was You who brought me here!"

Praise be to God, not only did He answer my plea to calm down my bowels immediately, but I also distinctly heard Him say to me, "You're not the smartest nor the brightest in this subject. Your angle is you're going to be the most vulnerable." And by vulnerability, I knew exactly He meant elaborating on my childhood family financial trauma to the room full of spiritual giants.

By the time it came to my turn to speak, I did just that. I told the group that my greatest hang up and weakness was money, because of the way I had lost my birthright. And the fact that there was a panel on Christian macroeconomics in this event, it legitimized the parallel of personal stewardship as being viewed as Christian microeconomics. I also explained how I saw my own journey as depicted in my white paper mirroring the precepts in Micah 6:8. I really felt the presence of the Holy Spirit with me in delivering that message so calmly, compared with the dire crisis I was facing minutes earlier. I ended up winning the Best White Paper in the Stewardship category.

The key message to me from this incredible affirmation was that even though I am a nobody with no qualifications and no credentials, if God chooses to work through me, and I am willing to cooperate, nothing is impossible.

The greatest gift I took away from CEF was neither the award nor the affirmation, however. Rather, it was the chance to meet two white Zimbabwean brothers who had been heavily persecuted by the Mugabe government. Sylvia and I had set aside a sum of money to spend at a Michelin-starred meal—but instead we felt moved by the Holy Spirit to give that money to the brothers to buy gifts for their families.

CHAPTER 15

SHANGHAI SURPRISE

IN HONG KONG EARLIER that year, the Stewardship Committee at my church was hoping to visit each Life Group and offer a session on the topic of money. It is a vital subject, but one that many of the volunteer leaders of these Bible study groups found difficult to discuss. My life story up to this point formed a neatly packaged 45-minute talk—and always triggered fascinated comments and questions. So, starting in September 2015, I began visiting different groups over the next few months to offer my journey with great vulnerability and humility. Thankfully, there were not any allergic reactions (at least not up front) after any of the Life Group visits, and at a minimum, seeds had been sown on this often swept aside, uncomfortable topic.

Instead of finding it a chore, going around to tell my story in hope of pointing others in the direction of God in the often taboo subject of money actually brought me a lot of joy.

In early 2016, I was due to go to Shanghai for a business trip, and I contacted a good friend of mine based there to see whether he was free to catch up over dinner or drinks. He mentioned that he had a Bible study that evening and asked whether I would be interested to join him and my brother-in-law, an invitation which I gladly accepted.

After I landed and got into a car, I felt moved by the Holy Spirit to share my journey with this group, which led me to ask my friend what the plan was for that evening. He said the usual format was dinner then followed by Bible study, but that evening he did not have time to prepare for any topics in advance so my 45-minute story would be perfect. Wonderful, I thought.

As I stepped into the restaurant, I expected the receptionist to direct me to a private room (after all, this was in China where I thought a little extra discretion was required), but instead she pointed at a large table smack in the middle of the restaurant! Then came the bigger surprise as I approached the table: I spotted a well-known Hong Kong billionaire amongst the fellow dinner guests! Now there were some fairly well-to-do folks at my church, but they were not at the same stratospheric level of wealth as this individual. I was feeling a bit nervous to be talking to this multi-billionaire about money, so I prayed, "God, please give me courage to not water down the message, and if anything, please give me more wisdom and insight which I can draw from my story." Sure enough, God is faithful, and the following concrete illustration was downloaded to me towards the tail end of my talk:

When people think about a blessed life, it usually evolves around long life and lots of money. Ever since Genesis 6:3, God has put a cap on human longevity, which to this day despite all the advancement in life sciences, still holds true:

Then the Lord said, "My Spirit will not contend with humans forever, for they are mortal; their days will be a hundred and twenty years."

The world's richest person is Bill Gates with a net worth of around US$90 billion (at the time of writing). Let's be generous—let's say God gave you US$120 billion at birth. Over a life span of 120 years, simple math would give you US$1 billion to spend a year. No need to worry about generating income or earning interest. You will have a tough time spending that amount of cash year after year.

Not that we could bring any money to the grave with us, but let's just say for argument's sake that you could. Let's say that you could bring US$120 billion with you to the other side of the grave, to heaven. Now here is the issue: how long is eternity? It is hard to imagine anything infinite, so, for practical purposes, let's think of a period which lasts a very long time—think about 120 Earth years with 120 zeros after that:

120,000,000,000,000,000,000,000,000,000,000,000,000,000,000,
000,000,000,000,000,000,000,000,000,000,000,000,000,000,000,
000,000,000,000,000,000,000,000,000

The same simple math that got you feeling so set for life with US$1 billion a year, how far would your US$120 billion get you now? The answer is:

US$0.00000000000000000000000000000000000000000000000000000
00000000000000000000000000000000000000000000000000000000000
000000000000001

That is a tiny fraction of a cent. You cannot even get a grain of rice with that. In finance-speak, with infinitely long duration in heaven, we need to be rich towards God in perpetual currency.

This could well be the deceitfulness of wealth which Jesus talked about in the Parable of the Sower (Matthew 13:22). In Revelation 3:17 it says:

"You say, 'I am rich; I have acquired wealth and do not need a thing.' But you do not realize that you are wretched, pitiful, poor, blind and naked."

We do need to be rich towards God because there must be a different kind of currency which is used for eternity. From the Parable of the Rich Fool in Luke 12 and the Parable of the Shrewd Manager in Luke 16, Luke 12:21 and Luke 16:11 clearly imply there is a difference between earthly wealth and eternal riches:

"This is how it will be with whoever stores up things for themselves but is not rich toward God."

"So if you have not been trustworthy in handling worldly wealth, who will trust you with true riches?"

If not viewed and handled correctly, money can very easily become our counterfeit God if life on Earth is the full extent of our worldview. In hindsight, God was gracious in giving me 15 to 16 times of practice in delivering the same message prior to this occasion, such that despite my nervousness, I was able to deliver it smoothly.

CHAPTER 16

SOUND CHECK

IF YOU WILL INDULGE me, I would like to share another true story, although I cannot remember exactly when this event took place, nor the name of the individual involved. But if my memory serves me correctly, it happened roughly two winters ago, either shortly before or after the Shanghai trip I mentioned in the previous chapter.

One Sunday at church, there was an empty seat to my right in the far end of the sanctuary, and a newcomer walked in almost halfway through the service, right before the sermon began. I noticed that he was carrying some kind of musical instrument case. Since I am some-what musical myself (I play the clarinet and egg shaker, though not at the same time), I made it a point to say hello to him after service.

As the sermon began, something else about this individual caught my eye—he brought out the most beat-up and underlined Bible I have ever seen, with so many notes written in the margins that it was nothing short of a miracle for anyone to be able to read from it.

He had a bit of a Kenny G type look to him, so it seemed fitting when I learned, after the service, that he was a saxophone player and that he was between gigs at the moment.

Thinking that our worship band could definitely use a professional saxophone player, I introduced him to the worship team playing that Sunday.

And then it happened.

I heard an unmistakable, audible voice in my head. "Give him money," it said.

This had NEVER happened to me before.

I knew right away that it was a message from God. I had to excuse myself from the conversation to pull out my wallet and check how much cash I had on me. I had HK$1,000 (worth approximately US$128) in the form of two HK$500 notes.

Essentially, I had three options: one, ignore the voice of God; two, give him HK$500; or three, empty my wallet for this total stranger. I picked the last option.

Not wanting to embarrass him, I pulled him aside and told him that there was some money I wanted him to have. He accepted the cash gratefully—which can be just as difficult, for many people, as giving cash away. After this, we chatted a bit more about his background (he was originally from Los Angeles), and whether he was likely to stay in Hong Kong (he was previously part of a jazz band on a cruise ship but had recently lost his regular gig, so he was playing saxophone in the streets).

Then came the spine shivering moment: this Bible-loving Christian man told me he came to our church that particular morning because God had told him that someone there would give him money. I was stunned and humbled at the same time for playing a role in this small miracle.

CHAPTER 17

FROM ASHES TO BEAUTY

IN THE EARLY summer of 2016, a very severe fire broke out in a mini-storage facility in Hong Kong. The first day of the fire claimed the life of a young fireman, and I was deeply moved by the news. Learning that he had a young family, I scrambled through different sources to see whether there was a way to donate money to financially assist the widow and their young baby. Within a few hours, the donation information became available, and immediately I shared the widow's account details on all my social media channels. I asked my mom and my sister to help, and they both generously agreed to chip in the same amount. With that, I topped it up to a nice round number and made the transfer to the widow's bank account. It felt good after reaching out to help this widow in distress (James 1:27).

Shortly afterwards, the fire sadly claimed another fireman's life. He, too, left behind a wife and a young son. I am a bit ashamed to admit this, but I did not feel as moved about the second fireman. So I debated what I should do, with questions like what if there were to be a third or a fourth fireman would I keep giving?

At a minimum, I thought I should go through the same routine—once again I blasted out the donation information on all my social media accounts appealing for donations, and then I approached my mom and my sister for the same conversation.

My mom graciously agreed to chip in the same amount, and even though my sister did not say anything, I did not blame her. When I stood in front of the ATM machine, the first thought that came to my mind was only God and I would ever know how much I gave to this second widow. As I was contemplating what number to punch in, I felt God was telling me to give the same amount, which meant I ended up personally giving more to the second widow (only now in hindsight it occurred to me that it was the same logic behind the Parable of the Vineyard Workers that perhaps He was trying to teach me—please refer to Matthew 20:1-16).

This nice round number in turn became my new lot size in donations, and subsequent to this tragic mini-storage fire I would find myself feeling really touched and moved by other news stories I would read about in the paper, where either the father figure or the primary breadwinner in the family passed away. Each time when I received the go ahead from God after asking Him whether to help or not, I would donate this new lot size to the charity fund set up by a local Hong Kong newspaper, which a good Buddhist friend of mine vouched for their integrity.

CHAPTER 18

ZERO INTEREST LOAN, TAKE TWO

SOME TIME AGO, I became friends with a family who relied solely on God for provision, and I was copied on their regular prayer requests. Around October the year before last, I learned that they had been falling behind in their rental payments, and they were going to be evicted around Christmas time by their landlord. Even though I felt empathetic towards their situation, there was a part of me that did not want to get involved, sensing that it was going to be messy, especially having just closed out the previous debt forgiveness episode two years earlier. However, God nudged me to write them a private email to ask them exactly how much rent they owed the landlord. I was a bit taken aback by how much rent they were paying, having visited their place before. After sitting on the knowledge over a weekend of how much was required to prevent eviction, the wife called me on my mobile phone. She was crying.

She asked me if I saw her husband's email. At that point, I freaked out and became really scared. Thankfully, the email was somewhat innocuous, but I asked myself why I was so afraid. The only explanation I could come up with was that I must have imagined how I would have felt knowing I could have prevented my worst fear from materializing i.e. the husband's email being a suicide note, due to the fact that I did not act upon helping them when it was within my ability to do so.

Over the years, I have built up some margin, so that I am financially in a position to help others who are in need. I was convicted by the teaching in James 4:17 which says "If anyone, then, knows the good they ought to do and doesn't do it, it is sin for them." Intuitively and culturally, it was neither the rational nor the smart thing to do, but from the standpoint of grace through the eyes of Jesus Christ, I could not say no despite knowing that this was a mere short term, stopgap solution.

Immediately, I decided to pay their four months' worth of outstanding rent. Having learned from the previous experience, I structured a six-month grace period before repayment started (the idea being they would have time to look for income-generating employment), with the zero-interest loan amortized over 40 months which the couple thought was a super generous offer and a workable repayment schedule. It earned me the right to speak into their lives, and subsequently they moved into a more affordable place to live. The six-month grace period went by quickly, and I checked in every now and then with this family to see how they were getting on.

Perhaps I was naively thinking that with the previous experience under my belt, nothing would surprise me. Clearly God had intended this to be further education for me. Unlike the previous experience where the first year's monthly repayments went like clockwork, on this occasion even the first installment repayment could not be serviced. It took me a lot of courage for me to step out of my comfort zone and visit this couple at their new home—not to harass them for repayment but to show genuine concern for their family, maintain the relationship and to keep them accountable, which was something I failed to do in the previous 2007-14 episode.

Within a year of this seemingly expensive act of mercy, God blessed me with over 100 times return on the amount I extended to this family. The financial gain came through a specific investment, which is a story in itself, one I will touch upon in a later chapter. I am neither making a direct correlation between my giveaway and my return, nor am I suggesting a cause and effect type explanation. This is simply a factual recount of what happened, not "prosperity gospel" which falsely preaches that good and faithful Christian living necessarily leads to an abundance of wealth. God is good to us, without expecting a return; we should be good to others, again without expecting a return.

Personally, I have a strong conviction that God has established His promises this way, as evidenced by Proverbs 19:17 which says "Whoever is kind to the poor lends to the Lord, and he will reward them for what they have done." Even so, our hearts need to be in the right place—we do not arbitrage our giving as a means to get rich.

My intention is to visit this family periodically and pray for them to generate sustainable income for their household, until the Year of Debt Forgiveness comes around.

CHAPTER 19

HEARING GOD

YOU MAY HAVE heard of Kenneth Bae, the Korean-American pastor who was jailed in North Korea for more than two years before being released. For details of his inspirational story, I highly recommend his book *Not Forgotten – The True Story of My Imprisonment in North Korea.*

In January last year, through the coordination of a Christian NGO which my wife Sylvia is a board member of, Kenneth came to speak at our church, and during that week I got to meet him several times. Feeling very moved by hearing his journey from being arrested to being released and the new global initiative he was planning to solicit around the clock prayers for North Korea and its people, I considered it a special privilege to lead worship that particular Sunday together with Sylvia. A few months later in May, Kenneth came back to Hong Kong, and we got invited to a small group dinner organized by a brother at church. Towards the end of dinner, while Kenneth was describing the blueprint for his new Seoul-based NGO, a very specific amount in US dollars popped into my head which I knew came from the Holy Spirit. It was a number that I was not at all comfortable to give away (it would have been another 18% of my annual base salary in addition to my tithe plus other givings, and that year I had virtually zero expectations of getting any year-end bonus). I recall immediately thinking (or should I say "hoping") that surely it would not be for me to bear all by myself. Given it was a relatively large sum, and on his ministry's pamphlet only PayPal was mentioned as the donation method, I asked Kenneth whether there was a more direct and efficient way of transferring money to his NGO's account. At that time, Kenneth did not even know how much funding he needed to raise, so I decided to keep quiet about the USD amount that I had just heard from God, partly because I wanted to ignore it.

Two months went by, and in July the brother who hosted dinner forwarded an email from Kenneth which detailed his plans, including how much his NGO needed to raise. It was EXACTLY the figure that was revealed to me during dinner two months ago.

On the one hand, it was really stunning to be affirmed membership in this exclusive spacetime-defying spiritual communication channel. On the other hand, it became a burden on my heart—I needed to see to it that this amount was raised. I immediately started a chat group with the other four families in attendance at dinner, and thankfully one of the dinner participants suggested dividing up the amount five ways equally to get it done. This gracious approach took the weight off my shoulders, as I rationalized that the calling I had heard was still being fulfilled (albeit corporately).

CHAPTER 20

OBEYING GOD

WITHOUT GOING INTO details, it soon became obvious to me that, for various reasons, any payment would have to be made directly to Kenneth Bae's NGO bank account in Seoul. It was not so much of a big deal to me that there was no tax deduction via this donation method, but what troubled my mind more was the potential personal risk to my family involved in associating with him via direct bank transfer. I prayed about it earnestly, and a sense of peace emerged. If this was going to be part of the persecution package which every Christian was destined to face according to Scripture, then so be it. We can take comfort from the fact that God has an infinite capacity to compensate for that, either here or in heaven. I thought of 1 Peter 4:12-16:

Dear friends, do not be surprised at the fiery ordeal that has come on you to test you, as though something strange were happening to you. But rejoice inasmuch as you participate in the sufferings of Christ, so that you may be overjoyed when his glory is revealed. If you are insulted because of the name of Christ, you are blessed, for the Spirit of glory and of God rests on you. If you suffer, it should not be as a murderer or thief or any other kind of criminal, or even as a meddler. However, if you suffer as a Christian, do not be ashamed, but praise God that you bear that name.

In mid-August last year, after I made a direct payment of one-fifth the amount to the account in Seoul, I checked with Kenneth and he confirmed receipt of the transfer. I reported back to the dinner chat group that the direct payment instructions indeed worked, and I reminded them that, for the avoidance of doubt, there were no tax deductions from a Hong Kong Inland Revenue perspective in donating directly to a South Korean NGO, hoping to encourage the others to fulfill the other four-fifths outstanding.

This matter weighed on my heart. I knew there was a possibility that there might still be a chunk of funding outstanding. A few weeks later, I bumped into the brother who proposed dividing the sum five ways and gently inquired if he had made his payment yet. Without hesitation, he promised that he would get around to it the following day. And sure enough, a miracle that resulted in praise and thanksgiving to God happened due to his faithfulness: the very day his payment arrived, bills for rent, salary and interior decoration were due, and Kenneth's NGO was able to make good on them. They prayed that God would provide for those bills on September 15th, and the money came through bang on schedule. I reported back to the dinner chat group this good news that our faithfulness met such a timely need. I did so partly in hope that this would spur others on to meet the full funding need. As of September 18th, the shortfall was two-fifths of the original amount.

The burden kept lingering in the back of my mind for some reason. I prayerfully checked in with Kenneth again on the 29th, but to my great dismay no other amounts had come in since the 15th.

At that point, I became resigned to the fact that I was meant to ensure this promise was fulfilled. I decided I should not piggyback off others who did not have the same connection to this number as I did. Upon this realization, I instructed my banker to transfer a further two-fifths of the original amount to meet the shortfall.

Thinking I had completed the mission assigned from God, I texted Kenneth and revealed to him for the first time what happened at dinner, and especially after the numerical confirmation from the email months later, I felt the urge to go the extra mile in meeting the need.

The text I got back from him was not at all what I had expected. Indeed, I was a bit miffed.

While on the one hand Kenneth gave thanks for my faithfulness in providing the money which the NGO's entire staff had been praying for, there was now an additional two-fifths of funding needed for their new English school, and one-fifth for their website and promotional materials which they were about to launch.

It felt like God was telling me to not nickel-and-dime Him, and just do as I had been told. The next morning, I emailed my banker and asked to amend the transfer from two-fifths to four-fifths.

This meant that I lived up to my end of the bargain—I had paid one-fifth of the sum in mid-August and was now paying an additional four-fifths.

Subsequently, on October 17th a sister from the dinner group made good on her pledge, and an additional one-fifth was transferred to Kenneth's NGO. This covered the outstanding shortfall.

To ensure accuracy in recounting this episode, I went back to my chat history and email records to relive the timing and sequence of events. Without a doubt, it was God's way of making me surrender and obey the original assignment given to me, and also to recognize that I was not the only game in town, with two other brothers and sisters required to answer their calling to meet the expanded need in aggregate.

There is a difference between hearing God and obeying God. In the movie "The Matrix", Morpheus said to his protégé Neo "there's a difference between knowing the path and walking the path." There was a purpose for the financial blessing that I received of more than 100 fold return since granting the second zero-interest loan to that family, not only to supply the capital for starting Nehemiah Global Initiative, but also to further bolster my trust in God, to know that He really honors His Word.

Since completing the donation no more than six weeks before I started writing this book, God has already blessed me with multiple times return on the amount I gave (once again, I need to stress that it is not the "prosperity gospel" theory that I am preaching, but simply celebrating the fact that God is generous and wants us to be generous).

The whole episode was a learning experience for me. The amount of money felt uncomfortable at first—but looking back, it seemed like a test of my faith. By overcoming my fear of scarcity in provision and personal safety, once again God reminded me that He is faithful, and that He honors His Word regarding generosity in 2 Corinthians 9:6-11:

Remember this: Whoever sows sparingly will also reap sparingly, and whoever sows generously will also reap generously. Each of you should give what you have decided in your heart to give, not reluctantly or under compulsion, for God loves a cheerful giver. And God is able to bless you abundantly, so that in all things at all times, having all that you need, you will abound in every good work. As it is written:

"They have freely scattered their gifts to the poor; their righteousness endures forever."

Now he who supplies seed to the sower and bread for food will also supply and increase your store of seed and will enlarge the harvest of your righteousness. You will be enriched in every way so that you can be generous on every occasion, and through us your generosity will result in thanksgiving to God.

In hindsight, I was foolish to think that God was going to give me an easy way out of the donation amount that had been earmarked for me, since I always go around telling people that God is much more interested in training our character than caring about our comfort level.

CHAPTER 21

EXPERIENCING GOD

IN EARLY OCTOBER last year, I felt a distinct lack of peace in my soul. It bothered me so much that I felt compelled to try something I had never done before: I took a Friday off from work to do a spiritual retreat by myself, specifically to seek guidance from God about my work situation. Out of a number of retreat center options available in Hong Kong, I chose one by the name of Bethany in Cheung Chau, located on an outlying island which I had never been to before. It was so unlike me to take a 40-minute ferry ride and then trek 20 minutes on the island to find this retreat center tucked up on a hill.

Kenneth Bae happened to be in town that day, and I actually invited him to come along with me, but he declined due to another appointment. So I set off for a day of solitude with God, not expecting anyone to interact with me at Bethany apart from possibly the receptionist. The hike was much more strenuous than I had antici-pated, and it took more like half an hour to finally find this place up on the hill.

The instruction was to call the person in charge upon arrival, but instead I was greeted by a retired, elderly couple from the UK who were frequent guests at Bethany. Even though they were complete strangers, we struck up a warm conversation. I told them about what had brought me to this spiritual retreat and an abbreviated version of my stewardship journey, including my recent friendship and interac-tion with Kenneth Bae.

They were extremely affirmative that I had been making myself open and available to God for His purposes, which was most comfort-ing and encouraging.

When they asked me if any Scripture spoke to me that day, I told them that nothing particular jumped out at me from my daily Bible reading routine (a chapter from the Old Testament, a chapter of Psalms, a chapter of Proverbs which corresponded to the date, and a chapter from the New Testament) which I did during the ferry ride to Cheung Chau. Somehow, I felt compelled to share my birthday verse with this couple, even though I had never met them before. I was born on February 12th, so throughout the 66 books in the whole Bible, the 12th verse of the 2nd chapter which most resonates with me is Ruth 2:12:

"May the Lord repay you for what you have done. May you be richly rewarded by the Lord, the God of Israel, under whose wings you have come to take refuge."

Shortly after our pleasant chat which lasted about 45 minutes, they informed me that the prayer chapel had been dismantled, but there were some guestrooms which they did not see why I could not use for my half-day retreat.

The lady led me down the hallway and turned to the guestroom across from theirs which had a sign saying "Barnabas" on the door. There was a single bed, a chair and a desk inside. She told me that I could feel free to use it for a few hours. Once I closed the door of the guest room, guess what I found? A sign that said "Ruth". It was the Ruth room, and a shiver ran up my spine. It felt like an amazingly incredible affirmation that God wanted to communicate this message to me. It was like the closing scenes of the movie "Interstellar", in which a father in another place in the spacetime continuum communicates with his daughter by showing her signs.

It reminded me of Hebrews 13:5:

Keep your lives free from the love of money and be content with what you have, because God has said,
> *"Never will I leave you;*
> *never will I forsake you."*

I am convinced that this was His way of telling me He has got my back, and that He is keeping a close eye monitoring my situation. He brought me to this place, arranged for me to meet people (in my view they could have been angels) who prompted me to bring up my personal verse from the Bible's Book of Ruth, and then led me to this chamber: the Ruth Room.

I knew then that God was my Provider. Enough said.

CHAPTER 22

PLEDGING THE BIGGEST
AND THE BEST

WHEN THE PRELIMINARY idea of Community Church eventually purchasing our own premises was first tossed around at the beginning of 2017, I wanted to contribute in a significant way. But how? I could either base my donation on my relatively limited cash resources—which would not make much of a dent in the bill for a building in the heart of the most expensive city on Earth—or I could do something more creative: I could pledge the upside (i.e. the profit) on half the position of my largest investment with the greatest growth prospects.

There was a particular investment which was originally one of four stocks that I stumbled upon on the back of recommendations from some American friends during the tech bubble. It morphed from a 3D graphics chip gaming play into the proxy for future growth in Artificial Intelligence. I just happened to be a bag lady style investor, never selling anything I have picked up, and by sheer grace it has gone up by more than 20 times in value since I first bought it. Compared with the original amount I was contemplating to commit in a cash pledge, the current mark-to-market on the upside for half the position has already exceeded it by four times.

Let me continue to be absolutely honest with you. Every now and then, I do swallow hard and think about how much will have been carved out of my net worth by pledging 50% of the eventual profit on my largest and most successful equity investment—especially since it has so much potential for further exponential growth. Each time one of these internal debates occur, I quickly get back to my senses after remembering that everything I have belongs to God, and that I am merely managing the assets on His behalf. The saying "It's better to be lucky than good" is certainly true in my case! Also, the Holy Spirit frequently reminds me of 2 Samuel 24:24 where King David said: "No, I insist on paying you for it. I will not sacrifice to the Lord my God burnt offerings that cost me nothing."

It is my honor and privilege to be so blessed to be in a position to give than to receive (Acts 20:35). In telling my story openly and publicly, my hope is that it may encourage you to take a further step— whether it is your first or your millionth step is of no concern—in unleashing your generosity.

CHAPTER 23

PUTTING MY MONEY
WHERE MY MOUTH IS

I FIRST FELT the calling to write a book about my stewardship journey probably around 18 months ago, but I kept putting it aside until I felt I had time on my hands to do so.

Two weeks after my "Interstellar"-like spiritual retreat, my business unit at work got shut down unexpectedly, and I was unceremoniously fired.

After the first 24 hours of shock and dismay from the experience, it started to dawn on me that it could be a blessing in disguise.

For starters, I now had time to write this book. The curious thing was that a Christian brother had sent me a prophetic email the day before I was let go from my job. I had mentioned to him that I wanted to write a book about my stewardship journey, and he wanted to encourage me to do so without delay as he felt it would be valuable to many people, particularly those living in financial capitals around the world.

Still, the loss of my job was unexpected and certainly could be described as a crisis situation. But how a person reacts to such events is very telling. In the past, I would have been really unhappy, worried and depressed. The first thing I would have done would have been to update my CV and send it off to all the headhunters and professional contacts I knew, so that I could start searching for a new job. I would have feared that my three months' worth of "gardening leave" pay and the minimum severance payment required by the Hong Kong authorities would soon run out. I would have been anxious to find a new source of income to cover my mortgage and household expenses, including my two children's school fees, and so on.

Instead, I made a totally counterintuitive, countercultural decision. I chose to write this book first before looking for options for my next gig. In just seven sittings, I produced the first draft. Considering the traumatic financial history in my childhood, something fundamental must have changed for the better inside me. And I was, and am, feeling really calm about it.

Lots of people have been asking what I was going to do next, but deep down I had a strong conviction that I had to write this book first, as my own way of fulfilling Matthew 6:33:

"But seek first His kingdom and his righteousness, and all these things will be given to you as well."

In addition to being an act of worship, I knew that being in a right relationship with God meant being properly connected to the ultimate source of unlimited supply for all my needs.

A well-meaning friend from church quipped that some people thought it was easy for me to talk about stewardship and generosity as a relatively well-paid banker. Now that I am out of a job, perhaps that perception will change, given that I now have the opportunity, pardon the pun, to put my money where my mouth is. The loss of employment means that I do not just talk about trusting in the Lord for provision because He is the God who provides, but I am living that truth.

Rushing to find another job would have helped only myself—but putting down my stewardship journey on paper could potentially be life-giving to many. After the journey that God has put me through so far, He Himself has taught me who my real provider is: Jehovah Jireh. Not a job, not an institution, not a stream of income.

INHERITANCE PLANNING

I MARRIED Sylvia in December 2009. In 2011, we were blessed with a wonderful child: her name is Danielle (before we knew her gender, we decided on the name of Daniel as one of our favorite characters in the Bible). In 2014, we three were blessed by the arrival of a delightful boy named Enoch (his namesake walked with God and pleased Him so much that he was taken up to heaven without experiencing death). I know that the best thing I could ever do for them financially is not to include them in my will, with limited assets that have limited ability to generate income, but to include them in the will of our infinitely rich and generous Heavenly Father. Proverbs 14:26 says: "Whoever fears the Lord has a secure fortress, and for their children it will be a refuge."

Hand on heart, I did not even recognize how this verse tied in with my birthday verse Ruth 2:12 until I was literally typing it in the book:

"May the Lord repay you for what you have done. May you be richly rewarded by the Lord, the God of Israel, under whose wings you have come to take refuge."

There is no place more secure in any respect than the refuge of the Lord.

I never would have thought that I would ever say this, but I thank God for lowering my income to teach me self-sacrifice and to condition me to a more sustainable yet still very comfortable lifestyle. I also thank Jesus for not giving me too much money, for it is said in Proverbs 30:7-9:

"Two things I ask of you, Lord; do not refuse me before I die: Keep falsehood and lies far from me; give me neither poverty nor riches, but give me only my daily bread. Otherwise, I may have too much and disown you and say, 'Who is the Lord?' Or I may become poor and steal, and so dishonor the name of my God."

Having excessive wealth may give us the false impression that we can sever our dependence on God. There is a Chinese saying "飲水

思源", which means "when you drink water, remember the source" (this, by the way, was supposedly a favorite saying of my late paternal grandfather, according to my dad). God warned the Israelites in Deuteronomy 8:18: "But remember the Lord your God, for it is He who gives you the ability to produce wealth, and so confirms His covenant, which He swore to your ancestors, as it is today."

Perhaps it is this kind of spiritual DNA and legacy I would like to pass down to my future generations, something that could not be stripped away from them like my tangible birthright in the form of a family business. The paint business that once meant the world to me, its owner recently tried to go for a spin-off initial public offering (IPO) in Hong Kong but did not go through due to a last-minute shareholder dispute. I know it does not bother me anymore because it did not cause too much of a stir in my emotions when reading about it in the press. I wish them the best of luck going forward.

After journeying for three decades since that traumatic financial event, I can now say to my relatives what Joseph said to his brothers who betrayed him in Genesis 50:20: "You intended to harm me, but God intended it for good to accomplish what is now being done, the saving of many lives." My message is intended to be used as a timely catalyst to stir up a rethink on generosity, which could potentially benefit many impoverished lives around the world.

God has turned my greatest hurt, my greatest weakness in the form of slavery to money into my greatest strength in gradually gaining mastery over it.

The more serious a student I have become of stewardship, the more I realize how much more there is to learn and to put into practice. Limitless is the best word I could come up with to describe it. And in terms of my earlier naivety in thinking that I have arrived after "mastering" the basics of tithing, to borrow from the rock band U2, I still haven't found what I'm looking for.

I now view my role as God's payment agent. Having lost my job in investment banking recently, I pray that I can sustain my willingness and ability to carry on this function for His glory and purpose. It would be tragic if I start becoming inwardly focused on meeting my own family's needs due to a scarcity mindset—please pray for me.

May this book be a blessing to you, leading you to discover and to trust our great Jehovah Jireh, the God who provides. This is my prayer for you:

Dear Lord and Heavenly Father,

I thank you for leading this reader to finish reading my story. I pray that a seed has been sown into his or her heart, and that You will help it grow. I pray that the reader will decide to take a step, even a baby step, in the direction of following Your nudging in the area of money, and may Your presence be felt so that they will know You are indeed Jehovah Jireh, the God who provides, and that they will be set free from slavery stemming from the deceitfulness of wealth.

May we all be released from our traditional mindset and assumption from classical microeconomics that resources are scarce, and allocation choices need to be made on that basis, so that we can become more daring in being generous on every occasion, because the richest King in the entire universe has promised to provide for us, His children, in doing His business to look after the poor and needy.

In Jesus's most precious name I pray,
Amen.

ACKNOWLEDGEMENTS

English was my weakest subject in high school and college. Sometimes I still have to pinch myself to believe that I have actually written a book.

There are numerous people to thank for getting this book to fruition, but above all it is Jesus Christ my Lord and Saviour, who has graciously molded my life journey to become a story for His glory and purpose. I thank Him for placing the following people in my life: Nury Vittachi for his encouragement and guidance throughout the process from start to finish; Gary Hoag for paving and leading the way on the endorsements front; Stephanie Cheung for pointing me in the direction of Elm Hill Books, and also for a painting which without a doubt will one day be used powerfully; my wife Sylvia in bearing with me and helping me with my weakest link on cover design; my parents Bill and Nancy for lovingly providing for me; and last, but not least, everyone who has taken valuable time to review my manuscript.

I have experienced more supernatural stories of provision since completing the final draft of my manuscript end of January this year. God willing, may these new life lessons learned be shared to the ends of the Earth in a format that most effectively glorifies Him. Amen.

CPSIA information can be obtained
at www.ICGtesting.com
Printed in the USA
LVOW11s1223110618

580305LV00001B/1/P